Williams Sonoma
April 14 /07
Lynnwood

Decorated Cookies

Decorated Cookies

Joanna Farrow

hamlyn

First published in Great Britain in 2006 by
Hamlyn, a division of Octopus Publishing Group Ltd
2–4 Heron Quays, London E14 4JP

Cars edition
ISBN-13: 978-0-600-61519-4

Reindeer edition
ISBN-13: 978-0-600-61612-2

A CIP catalogue for this book is available from
the British Library

Printed and bound in China

10 9 8 7 6 5 4 3 2 1

notes

A few recipes include nuts or nut derivatives. It is
advisable for those with known allergic reactions to nuts
and nut derivatives and those who may be potentially
vulnerable to these allergies, such as pregnant and
nursing mothers, invalids, the elderly, babies and
children, to avoid dishes made with nuts and nut
oils. It is also prudent to check the labels of prepared
ingredients for the possible inclusion of nut derivatives.

The FDA advises that eggs should not be consumed
raw. This book contains some recipes made with raw
or lightly cooked eggs. It is prudent for more vulnerable
people such as pregnant and nursing mothers, invalids,
the elderly, babies and young children to avoid
uncooked or lightly cooked dishes made with eggs.

Whole milk should be used unless otherwise stated.
Large eggs should be used unless otherwise stated.
Ovens should be preheated to the specified
temperature—if using a fan-assisted oven, follow
the manufacturer's instructions for adjusting the
time and the temperature.

contents

introduction

When it comes to teatime treats, nothing quite compares to a batch of delicious homemade cookies. The unmistakable aroma fills the house and, if you're not careful, the cookies might not last much beyond the cooling rack, as family members swarm around the kitchen, eager to have a taste. As they're a favorite with kids, cookies are also a great way to get children interested in cooking and to learn some basic skills, under supervision. And the fun's not over when the cookie dough is prepared: in fact, it's only just beginning. There are decisions to be made about what shapes to cut out, how to decorate them, and what colors to use—and then, of course, you get to eat them!

The wonderful thing about baking and decorating your own cookies is that you can tailor them to any occasion, and the recipes here will give you plenty of

decorating with royal icing

1 Some cookies are decorated with an outline of royal icing. Use the recipe on page 16. Once it's made, transfer a small amount to a pastry bag. Holding the bag at an angle, pipe the icing around the edge of the cookie to make an outline. Allow this to set for a few minutes.

2 Add a few drops of cold water to the icing and beat so that it forms a flat surface when left to stand for 15 seconds. Spoon into the center of the cookie and use a small spatula to smooth it over the surface, up to the border. On a very small area, flood the icing from a paper pastry bag with the tip snipped off onto the cookie, filling any corners with a toothpick or skewer.

3 Once you've iced all the cookies, set them aside for 1–2 hours so that the icing can dry sufficiently before you add the next layer of decorations or other detail.

inspiration. There are ideas for Easter, Halloween, and Christmas, as well as plenty of designs that would be perfect for birthdays and other special events. Certain doughs are used for a number of the recipes and you'll find these at the beginning of the book for easy reference. This also means that you can prepare more than one batch of dough at a time and freeze the surplus until you're ready to bake and decorate more cookies.

basic techniques

Many of the recipes use an icing layer on the cookie as a base for the design. There are two distinct techniques for applying this and it really depends on whether you want to use royal icing or a ready-to-use icing. Once the icing has set, it works as a kind of easel on which you can paint or trace your design, or add other decorations or details.

decorating with ready-to-use icing

1 Bake your cookies and wait until they have cooled before you begin. Roll out the icing to the required thickness. If you used cookie cutters for your cookies, then use these to cut out the icing so that you'll have the exact shape. If you didn't use cutters, then you can rest a cookie over the icing and cut around it.

2 To secure the icing to the cookies, use a spatula or the back of a spoon to spread a little fruit glaze, melted chocolate, or royal icing (as stated in the recipe) onto the cookie, then place the icing onto it.

3 Other fondant shapes or decorations can now be placed on top of the icing base to complete your design.

planning a party

A cookie-decorating party is a wonderful idea for a child's birthday. However, it isn't just kids who enjoy getting messy—there's a great feeling of satisfaction to be had from creating your own cookie designs and a decorating party would be ideal for a family gathering, a house-warming, or a seasonal get-together. Homemade cookies also make lovely gifts, so you might consider gathering a group of friends together and making batches of cookies to give away at Easter or Christmas.

If you haven't hosted a cookie-decorating party in your home before, there are a few useful tips to help the event run smoothly and ensure that everyone has a good time.

* If you're inviting a lot of people, consider asking them to bring their own homemade or bought cookies with them to decorate. With fewer people, you'll probably want to bake your own, but again, do this in advance.
* If the occasion is a children's party, why not have a theme? This will help to focus the kids' attention and make the preparation easier. You could have a pirate party: bake the cookies in advance (see recipe on page 42) and, if you're feeling adventurous, you could also decorate the room in a pirate theme and ask the kids to come in fancy dress.
* Cover all surfaces that are going to be used for decorating and remove any valuable or delicate objects from the room where you're going to set up the decorating station—you don't want costly accidents!
* Make sure everything's set up well in advance so that you don't have to waste time searching through cabinets during the party. This means preparing different-colored icings and checking that you have plenty of sprinkles, candies, and other decorations for your guests to choose from.
* Check that you've got plenty of utensils for everyone—if you don't have enough, ask family members or neighbors to lend you extra pastry bags, spatulas, and so on.
* Buy little bags or cake boxes so that your guests can take home some of their creations. This is particularly important for children's parties, as the kids will be desperate to show off their carefully decorated cookies to proud parents!

essential equipment

Cookie baking and decorating doesn't require too much in the way of specialist utensils and, if you bake a lot, you'll probably already have everything you need. Here's a list of some of the basic items of equipment to get you started:

* Cookie sheets
* Cookie cutters (choose shapes that can be used for different occasions)
* Pastry bags and tips (a variety of different-size tips is essential)
* Rolling pin
* Spatula
* Tape measure
* Small, sharp knife or scalpel (for cutting icing and fondant shapes)
* Paintbrush (for intricate artwork)
* Strainer or sifter
* Skewers and toothpicks

basic recipes

Here are all the basic cookie recipes that are used in the decorated cookie chapters, so refer to the chosen recipe for how to cut out and bake the dough.

spicy gingerbread

½ cup unsalted butter, softened, plus extra
   for greasing
½ cup light brown sugar
1 egg, beaten
⅓ cup molasses
3 cups self-rising flour, plus extra for
   dusting
1½ teaspoons ground ginger

Makes about 24
Preparation time: 10 minutes, plus chilling
Cooking time: 15 minutes

Beat together the butter and sugar until creamy. Stir in the egg and molasses. Sift the flour and ginger into the bowl and stir in with a wooden spoon to form a stiff paste.

Turn the dough out onto a lightly floured countertop and knead lightly until smooth. Wrap and chill for at least 30 minutes before using.

Roll out the dough on a lightly floured surface and, using cookie cutters, cut out shapes. Place on greased cookie sheets, spaced slightly apart, and bake in a preheated oven, 350°F, for 15 minutes or until the dough has risen slightly and is beginning to darken around the edges. Leave on the cookie sheets to cool.

vanilla cookies

2½ cups all-purpose flour, plus extra for
  dusting

1 cup firm unsalted butter, cut into small
  pieces, plus extra for greasing

1 cup confectioners' sugar

2 egg yolks

2 teaspoons vanilla extract

Makes about 20
Preparation time: 10 minutes, plus chilling
Cooking time: 15 minutes

This is a really buttery cookie dough with a subtle vanilla flavor.
It's particularly versatile, going well with most frostings and toppings.

Put the flour in a food processor and add the butter. Whiz until the mixture
resembles fine bread crumbs.

Add the sugar, egg yolks, and vanilla extract and whiz to a smooth dough.
Wrap and chill for at least 30 minutes before using.

Roll out the dough on a lightly floured surface and, using cookie cutters,
cut out shapes. Place them on greased cookie sheets, spaced slightly apart,
and bake in a preheated oven, 350°F, for 15 minutes or until pale golden.
Leave on the cookie sheets to cool.

Variation:
Chocolate cookies Replace ¼ cup flour with cocoa powder.

piped cookies

¾ cup unsalted butter, very soft,
  plus extra for greasing

¼ cup superfine sugar

1 teaspoon vanilla extract

2 cups all-purpose plain flour

1 tablespoon milk

Makes about 12

Preparation time: 10 minutes

Cooking time: 20 minutes

This dough makes quite a firm paste, so it might be easier to pipe half the quantity at a time.

Beat together the butter, sugar, and vanilla extract until very pale and creamy. Add the flour and milk and mix to form a smooth paste.

Put the mixture in a large pastry bag fitted with a large star or plain tip. Pipe fingers, rings, or squiggles of dough, spaced slightly apart, onto 2 greased cookie sheets.

Bake in a preheated oven, 350°F, for 15–20 minutes or until slightly risen and just beginning to darken. Using a spatula, transfer to a wire rack to cool.

chunky oat cookies

½ cup unsalted butter, plus extra
  for greasing
½ cup superfine sugar
1 tablespoon corn syrup
1 cup rolled oats
1 cup self-rising flour
½ teaspoon baking soda

Makes about 12
Preparation time: 10 minutes, plus cooling
Cooking time: 25 minutes

This quick and easy cookie mixture is rolled into balls and then flattened slightly on the cookie sheet so that they spread a little during baking.

Put the butter, sugar, and corn syrup into a saucepan and heat gently until the butter has melted. Remove from the heat and stir in the oats, flour, and baking soda until well mixed. Tip into a bowl and leave for a few minutes until cool enough to handle.

Shape heaping teaspoonfuls of the mixture into balls and place on a large, greased cookie sheet, spacing them well apart. Flatten each slightly with the back of a fork and bake in a preheated oven, 350°F, for 15–20 minutes until the cookies have spread slightly and are pale golden. Using a spatula, transfer to a wire rack to cool.

wafer snaps (pictured right)

2 tablespoons unsalted butter, melted,
  plus extra for greasing

3 egg whites

⅓ cup superfine sugar

⅓ cup all-purpose flour

2 tablespoons light cream

Makes 18–20
Preparation time: 15 minutes
Cooking time: 8 minutes

Line 2 cookie sheets with parchment paper and lightly grease the paper. Beat together the egg whites and sugar until the egg whites are broken up. Stir in the melted butter, flour, and cream to form a smooth paste.

Spoon 6 scant tablespoonfuls of the paste, spaced well apart, onto the paper and spread each with the back of the spoon to a round, about 2½ inches in diameter.

Bake in a preheated oven, 375°F, for 7–8 minutes or until the edges are turning golden. Peel the cookies off the paper and place over a rolling pin to set before transferring to a wire rack.

Make more cookies using the remaining paste. (If they've started to harden on the cookie sheet before you've had a chance to shape them, pop them back in the oven very briefly to soften.)

biscotti

¼ cup lightly salted butter, softened, plus
  extra for greasing

¼ cup superfine sugar

1½ cups self-rising flour, plus extra for dusting

1 teaspoon baking powder

½ teaspoon ground coriander

finely grated zest of 1 orange, plus
  1 tablespoon juice

⅓ cup cornmeal

1 egg, lightly beaten

⅔ cup unblanched almonds, roughly chopped

Makes about 28
Preparation time: 20 minutes, plus cooling
Cooking time: 50 minutes

Beat together the butter and sugar until creamy. Add the flour, baking powder, coriander, orange zest and juice, cornmeal, and egg and mix to form a firm dough. Knead in the nuts.

Turn the dough out on a lightly floured surface and knead lightly until evenly mixed. Divide the mixture in half and shape each piece into a log about 9 inches long. Place on a large, greased cookie sheet, spacing them well apart, and flatten each to a depth of about ¾ inch.

Bake in a preheated oven, 325°F, for 30–35 minutes or until risen and just firm. Leave on the cookie sheet to cool for 15 minutes, then transfer to a board and, using a serrated knife, cut across into ½ inch thick slices.

Arrange on the cookie sheet, cut sides down, and bake for an additional 10–15 minutes until crisp. Using a spatula, transfer to a wire rack to cool.

icings, frostings, and glazes

royal icing

1 egg white

2 cups confectioners' sugar

Preparation time: 3 minutes

If not using immediately, cover the surface of the icing with plastic wrap so that it doesn't form a crust. It keeps well in the refrigerator for several days. Beat it with a wooden spoon before use, adding a drop of lemon juice or water if the icing has thickened.

Using a hand-held electric beater, beat the egg white with a little of the sugar until smooth.

Gradually beat in the remaining sugar until softly peaking. Turn into a small bowl and cover until ready to use.

citrus glaze

4 teaspoons lemon, lime, or orange juice

1 cup confectioners' sugar

Preparation time: 2 minutes

Use lemon, lime, or orange juice in this simple glaze. Lemon and lime taste particularly good, as their sharp flavor helps balance the sweetness of the sugar. This glaze keeps well in the refrigerator for several days.

Put the citrus juice in a small bowl and gradually beat in the sugar until the glaze thickly coats the back of the spoon.

Cover the surface of the glaze with plastic wrap to prevent a crust forming and store in the refrigerator until ready to use.

butter frosting

¼ cup unsalted butter, softened

1 cup confectioners' sugar

1 tablespoon milk or cream

Preparation time: 3 minutes

This is a soft, creamy frosting that never sets hard, so is best used to decorate cookies that won't be stacked up (unless you're using the frosting to sandwich two cookies together). Use the frosting plain, or add one of the flavor variations below.

Beat the butter and a little of the sugar together.

Gradually beat in the remaining sugar and the milk or cream until smooth. Cover and store in the refrigerator until ready to use.

Variations:
Vanilla Beat in 1 teaspoon vanilla extract.
Citrus Beat in 1 teaspoon finely grated orange, lemon, or lime zest and use juice instead of the milk or cream.
Coffee Dissolve 2 teaspoons instant coffee granules in 1 tablespoon boiling water and use instead of the milk or cream.

fruit glaze

6 heaping tablespoons good-quality jelly, such as strawberry, raspberry, or apricot

1 tablespoon water

Preparation time: 2 minutes

A simple glaze made using jelly adds gloss and color to decorated cookies and can be spread or piped from a tip. It keeps well in the refrigerator for several days.

Press the jelly through a strainer into a small saucepan.

Stir in the water and heat very gently until smooth. Allow the glaze to cool before using.

anytime cookies

thumbprint cookies

½ cup unsalted butter, softened, plus extra
   for greasing
¼ cup light brown sugar
1 egg, separated
½ teaspoon ground mixed spice
1 cup all-purpose flour
½ cup slivered almonds, crushed
5 tablespoons strawberry or raspberry jelly
confectioners' sugar, for dusting (optional)

Makes about 14
Preparation time: 20 minutes
Cooking time: 20 minutes

These are called "thumbprint" because you impress a thumbprint into each cookie to make a little cavity for the jelly filling. Peanut butter or chocolate spread make equally good alternatives to jelly.

Grease a large cookie sheet. Beat together the butter and brown sugar until creamy. Add the egg yolk, spice, and flour and mix until combined. Lightly beat the egg white to break it up and tip it onto a plate. Scatter the almonds on a separate plate.

Shape the cookie dough into small balls, about 1¼ inches in diameter, and roll them first in the egg white and then in the almonds until well coated.

Place the balls on the cookie sheet, spaced slightly apart, and flatten slightly. Bake in a preheated oven, 350°F, for 10 minutes, then remove from the oven. Allow to cool slightly, then lightly flour your thumb and make a thumbprint in the center of each cookie. Spoon a little jelly into each cavity and return the cookies to the oven for an additional 10 minutes or until pale golden. Using a spatula, transfer to a wire rack to cool. Dust the edges of the cookies with confectioners' sugar if desired.

fruit and nut cookies (pictured right)

butter, for greasing

1 quantity Chunky Oat Cookie dough
(see page 13)

⅓ cup mixed dried small soft fruits, such
as cranberries, blueberries, currants,
and strawberries

4 candied cherries, chopped

1 tablespoon pumpkin seeds

2 tablespoons slivered almonds

Makes 12
Preparation time: 20 minutes, plus cooling
Cooking time: 15 minutes

Grease a large sheet. Shape the cookie dough into 12 balls and flatten each until about 3¼ inches in diameter. Place on the cookie sheet, spacing them well apart.

Scatter the dried fruit in a circle around the edges of the cookies, then top the dried fruit with the cherries, pumpkin seeds, and slivered almonds to make a garland. Bake in a preheated oven, 350°F, for 15 minutes or until risen and pale golden. Using a spatula, transfer to a wire rack to cool.

frosted fruit cookies

butter, for greasing

1 quantity Vanilla Cookie dough, chilled
(see page 11)

flour, for dusting

1 egg white

2 cups mixture of red currants, black
currants, and white currants

⅔ cup blueberries

⅓ cup superfine sugar

1¼ cups heavy or whipping cream

2 teaspoons vanilla extract

Makes 20
Preparation time: 30 minutes, plus chilling
Cooking time: 15 minutes

Grease a large cookie sheet. Thinly roll out the cookie dough on a lightly floured surface and, using a 3¼ inch fluted, round cookie cutter, cut out rounds. Place on the cookie sheet, spacing them slightly apart, and re-roll the trimmings to make extras. Bake in a preheated oven, 350°F, for 15 minutes or until pale golden. Using a spatula, transfer to a wire rack to cool.

Lightly beat the egg white in a shallow dish to break it up. Leave 20 little clusters of the currants on their stalks for decoration and remove the rest by running them through the tines of a fork.

Brush all the fruits, including the clusters, with the egg white and then sprinkle with the sugar. Place on a parchment paper-lined tray or cookie sheet and leave to dry out for at least 30 minutes.

Whip the cream with the vanilla extract and pipe or spoon onto the cookies. Pile the sugar-frosted fruits onto the cream and place a cluster of currants on top of each for decoration.

chocolate florentines

¼ cup unsalted butter, plus extra
    for greasing

¼ cup light brown sugar

1 tablespoon heavy cream

⅓ cup pistachio nuts, skinned and chopped

½ cup slivered almonds

3 tablespoons candied cherries, chopped

3 tablespoons raisins

2 tablespoons all-purpose flour

vegetable oil, for greasing

3 oz bittersweet chocolate, broken up

3 oz milk chocolate, broken up

Makes 14
Preparation time: 25 minutes, plus setting
Cooking time: 12 minutes

Grease 2 cookie sheets. Melt the butter in a saucepan and stir in the sugar until dissolved. Bring to a boil, then remove from the heat. Stir in the cream, pistachio nuts, almonds, cherries, raisins, and flour and mix well.

Place heaping teaspoonfuls of the mixture on the cookie sheets, spacing them well apart. Bake in a preheated oven, 350°F, for 8–10 minutes, swapping the sheets over halfway through, until the cookies are golden, bubbling, and spreading.

Remove from the oven and, using an oiled round cookie cutter, push the edges of each cookie into the center to give a neat round edge. Return to the oven for 2 minutes. Leave on the cookie sheets until beginning to firm up, then use a spatula to transfer them to a wire rack to cool completely.

Melt the chocolate in 2 separate bowls. Line a cookie sheet with parchment paper. Dip the edges of the cookies in the chocolate—half in bittersweet, half in milk—and leave on the parchment paper in a cool place to set for about 1 hour.

stenciled cookies

butter, for greasing

1 quantity Spicy Gingerbread dough,
  chilled *(see page 10)*

flour, for dusting

1 quantity Butter Frosting *(see page 17)*

confectioners' sugar, for dusting

Makes 10

Preparation time: 25 minutes, plus chilling

Cooking time: 12 minutes

Design your own stencil for these cookies or, if you're short of time, use a paper doily to pattern the tops of the cookies after baking. The cookies will keep, stored in an airtight container, for up to one day.

Grease 2 cookie sheets. Thinly roll out the cookie dough on a lightly floured surface and, using a 2½ inch round cookie cutter, cut out rounds. Place on the cookie sheets, spacing them slightly apart, and re-roll the trimmings to make extras. Bake in a preheated oven, 350°F, for 12 minutes or until the dough has risen slightly and is beginning to darken around the edges. Using a spatula, transfer to a wire rack to cool.

Sandwich the cookies together with the butter frosting.

Make a template by cutting out a design, using a scalpel, on a 3 inch round of paper. Curvy lines, dots, numbers, and figures all look effective.

Lay the template over a cookie and dust with plenty of confectioners' sugar. Carefully lift the template away, shake off the excess sugar and repeat the decoration on the other cookies.

triple chocolate biscotti

butter, for greasing

1 quantity Biscotti dough (see page 14)

flour, for dusting

½ cup milk chocolate chips

5 oz bittersweet chocolate, broken up

2 oz white chocolate, broken up

Makes about 28

Preparation time: 35 minutes, plus cooling
and setting

Cooking time: 45 minutes

Traditionally, Italian biscotti are served with a dessert wine. This chocolate version is better suited to serving with tea or coffee.

Grease a large cookie sheet. Turn the dough out on a lightly floured surface and gently work in the chocolate chips until evenly combined. Divide the mixture in half and shape each into a log about 9 inches long. Place on the cookie sheet, spacing them well apart, and flatten slightly.

Bake in a preheated oven, 325°F, for 30 minutes or until risen and just firm. Leave on the cookie sheet to cool for 15 minutes, then transfer to a board and, using a serrated knife, cut across into ½ inch thick slices.

Arrange on the cookie sheet, cut sides down, and bake for an additional 15 minutes until crisp. Using a spatula, transfer to a wire rack and leave to cool.

Melt the bittersweet and white chocolate in 2 separate bowls. Line a tray or clean cookie sheet with parchment paper. Dip about one-third of each biscotti in the bittersweet chocolate, letting the excess fall back into the bowl. Place each cookie on the parchment paper.

Using a teaspoon, drizzle thin lines of white chocolate back and forth over the bittersweet chocolate to decorate. Leave in a cool place to set for about 1 hour.

linzer cookies

butter, for greasing

1 quantity Chunky Oat Cookie dough
(see page 13)

4 tablespoons raspberry jelly

9 oz white almond paste

confectioners' sugar, for dusting

Makes 12

Preparation time: 30 minutes, plus cooling

Cooking time: 17 minutes

Grease a large cookie sheet. Shape the cookie dough into 12 balls. Place on the cookie sheet, spacing them well apart, and flatten each slightly. Bake in a preheated oven, 350°F, for 15 minutes.

Spread a teaspoonful of jelly over the center of each cookie. Thinly roll out the almond paste on a surface lightly dusted with confectioners' sugar and, using a 3¼ inch round cookie cutter, cut out 12 rounds. Use a 2 inch round cutter to cut out the center of each round. Re-roll the trimmings and cut into ¼ inch wide strips. Cut each strip into 2 inch lengths.

Arrange 4 strips over each cookie to make a diamond pattern and place a round of paste over the top. Cook under a preheated broiler for about 2 minutes until golden, watching closely as the almond paste will brown very quickly.

Using a spatula, transfer to a wire rack to cool and dust the edges of the cookies with confectioners' sugar.

chocolate ring cookies

butter, for greasing

1 quantity Chocolate Cookie dough, chilled
  (see page 11)

flour, for dusting

4 oz white chocolate, broken up

3 oz bittersweet chocolate, in a block

½ cup unblanched hazelnuts, roughly
  chopped

crystallized rose petals

Makes 16

**Preparation time: 40 minutes, plus chilling
  and setting**

Cooking time: 15 minutes

Grease 2 cookie sheets. Roll out the cookie dough on a lightly floured surface and, using a 3¼ inch plain or fluted, round cookie cutter, cut out rounds. Using a 1¼ inch round cutter, cut out the centers to make rings. Place on the cookie sheets, spacing them slightly apart, and re-roll the trimmings to make extras. Bake in a preheated oven, 350°F, for 15 minutes or until beginning to darken around the edges. Using a spatula, transfer to a wire rack to cool.

Melt the white chocolate in a small bowl. Using a potato peeler, pare off curls from the bittersweet chocolate.

Using a teaspoon, drizzle a little white chocolate over one cookie and scatter with some hazelnuts, rose petals, and chocolate curls. Repeat with the other cookies. Leave in a cool place to set for about 1 hour.

gingerbread men

butter, for greasing

1 quantity Spicy Gingerbread dough,
    chilled *(see page 10)*

flour, for dusting

1 quantity Butter Frosting *(see page 17)*

3 oz each of red, orange, yellow, and pink
    ready-to-use icing

confectioners' sugar, for dusting

Makes 10–12
Preparation time: 1 hour, plus chilling
Cooking time: 15 minutes

Grease 2 cookie sheets. Roll out the cookie dough on a lightly floured surface and, using a gingerbread-man cutter about 5 inches in length, cut out figures. Place on the cookie sheets, spacing them slightly apart, and re-roll the trimmings to make extras. Bake in a preheated oven, 350°F, for 15 minutes or until the dough has risen slightly and is beginning to darken around the edges. Using a spatula, transfer to a wire rack to cool.

Put the butter frosting in a pastry bag fitted with a writer tip (or use a paper pastry bag and snip off the tip). Thinly roll out half of each icing color on a surface lightly dusted with confectioners' sugar. Using a ¼–½ inch flower plunger cutter, stamp out tiny flower shapes.

Re-roll the icing trimmings, along with the reserved half of each color, and cut out "shorts" or "sarongs." Position on the cookies, securing with a little butter frosting. Secure garlands of the flowers around the necks of the cookies with butter frosting and finish by piping faces with the frosting and outlining the "shorts" and "sarongs."

shoes and purses

butter, for greasing

1 quantity Vanilla Cookie dough, chilled
  (see pages 11)

flour, for dusting

1 quantity Royal Icing (see page 16)

a few drops of pink or lilac liquid or paste
  food coloring

a selection of tiny pink candies or cake
  decorations

Makes 20

**Preparation time: 1¼ hours, plus chilling
  and setting**

Cooking time: 15 minutes

**These are the perfect cookies for any "girly" gathering. They're great fun
to make and, of course, can be personalized both in color and design.**

Trace and cut out the shoe and purse templates on pages 94–95. Grease
2 cookie sheets. Roll out the cookie dough on a lightly floured surface. Lay
the templates over the dough and, using a small, sharp knife or scalpel, cut
around them. Place on the cookie sheets, spacing them slightly apart, and
re-roll the trimmings to make extras. Bake in a preheated oven, 350°F, for
15 minutes or until pale golden. Using a spatula, transfer to a wire rack
to cool.

Put a little of the icing in a pastry bag fitted with a fine writer tip. Divide
the remaining icing between 2 bowls. Add the food coloring to one bowl.
Stir a few drops of water into each bowl until the icing forms a flat surface
when left to stand for 15 seconds.

Use the icing in the bag to pipe an outline around each cookie, slightly
away from the edges, then add additional lines of piping for heels, soles,
and tops of boots.

Using a small teaspoon, drizzle a little of the colored icing onto one cookie,
easing it to the edges with the back of the spoon. Use a toothpick to push
the icing right into the corners. Repeat on all the remaining cookies so that
some are covered in colored icing, while others are in white. Before the
icing dries, gently press the candies into them to decorate. Leave in a cool
place to set for about 1 hour or until just dry to the touch.

Use the remaining icing in the bag to pipe additional decorations on the
cookies, such as flowers and borders on the purses and piping around the
tops of the shoes.

window boxes

1 quantity Vanilla Cookie dough, chilled
  (see page 11)
flour, for dusting
8 oz colored boiled candies
1 quantity Royal Icing (see page 16)
10 chocolate flake bars
a selection of small candies
sugar sprinkles

Makes 10
**Preparation time: 1 hour, plus chilling
  and setting**
Cooking time: 12 minutes

Once you've had fun decorating these cookies, arrange them on the windowsill so that the daylight can shine through the "glass."

Line 2 cookie sheets with parchment paper. Roll out the cookie dough on a lightly floured surface. Cut out 4 x 3¼ inch rectangles and transfer to the lined cookie sheets. Using a 1¼ inch square cutter, cut out 4 squares from one end of each rectangle to resemble window panes. Re-roll the trimmings and make more window shapes so that you end up with 10 window-shaped cookies.

Place on the cookie sheets and put a boiled candy in each cut-out square. Bake in a preheated oven, 350°F, for 12 minutes or until the cookies are beginning to color and the candies have melted to fill the squares. If necessary, ease the melted candies into the corners with a toothpick. Leave to cool on the cookie sheets.

Put the icing in a pastry bag fitted with a writer tip (or use a paper pastry bag and snip off the tip). Pipe a little icing onto the back of each chocolate flake bar and secure one along the base of each cookie. Make sure the chocolate sits right along the base of the cookie so that it can support the cookie in an upright position.

Use the icing in the bag to add little flower petals and trailing leaves around the windows, pressing a small candy into the centers. Fill the gaps with areas of dotted icing, sprinkling these with sugar sprinkles. Leave in a cool place to set for about 1 hour before standing the cookies upright.

magic wands

butter, for greasing

a few drops each of yellow and orange
 liquid food coloring

1 quantity Piped Cookie paste
 (see page 12)

1 quantity Royal Icing *(see page 16)*

different-colored sugar sprinkles

edible silver balls

Makes 14

Preparation time: 25 minutes, plus setting

Cooking time: 15 minutes

These little wands are made using a crisp, piped cookie mixture, so they won't stand too much waving around!

Grease 2 cookie sheets. Divide the cookie paste in two and stir the yellow food coloring into one half and the orange coloring into the other. Put the cookie paste into 2 large pastry bags fitted with plain tips.

Pipe fingers of paste onto the cookie sheets, each about 5 inches long. Bake in a preheated oven, 350°F, for 15 minutes or until slightly risen and just beginning to darken. Leave on the cookie sheets to cool for 5 minutes, then use a spatula to transfer them to a wire rack to cool completely.

Spread a little royal icing over one end of each cookie and scatter with plenty of sugar sprinkles and silver balls. Leave in a cool place to set for about 1 hour.

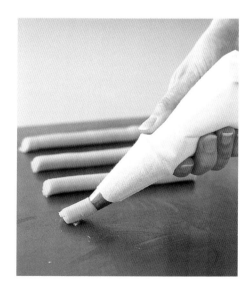

kids' cookies

pirates

strawberry or raspberry jelly

12 Chunky Oat Cookies *(see page 13)*

12 strawberry or licorice-flavored laces

5 oz black ready-to-use icing

confectioners' sugar, for dusting

3 oz white ready-to-use icing

3½ oz red ready-to-use icing

7 oz blue ready-to-use icing

small gold foil-wrapped chocolate coins

Makes 12

Preparation time: 40 minutes, plus cooling

Cooking time: 25 minutes

Supply the kids with all the decorating ingredients they need and leave them to experiment with creating their own pirate faces—each one is sure to be very different!

Spread a thin layer of jelly around one half of the edge of each cookie and secure a scrunched-up lace to each one for hair.

Roll out the black icing on a surface lightly dusted with confectioners' sugar and cut out eye patches. Secure to the cookies with a little jelly and add a long, thin strip of black icing to go over the patches and around the hair.

Using a little white and black icing, shape and position small eyes. Thinly roll out the red icing and cut out mouth shapes. Secure to the cookies with a little jelly and add tiny triangles of white and black trimmings for goofy teeth on some of the faces. Position a small gold coin on one side of some of the faces to represent an earring.

Roll out the blue icing on a surface lightly dusted with confectioners' sugar and dot with little balls of white icing. Gently roll with a rolling pin so the white icing blends into the blue to make a spotted pattern. Shape small headscarves and secure to some of the pirates. Use the trimmings to shape little knots at one end.

steam trains

butter, for greasing

1 quantity Vanilla Cookie dough, chilled
 (see page 11)

flour, for dusting

double quantity Butter Frosting
 (see page 17)

a few drops of blue, green, orange, or
 red liquid food coloring

large round candies for wheels

a selection of small candies, chopped

2 flat licorice-flavored laces

Makes 16

Preparation time: 50 minutes, plus chilling

Cooking time: 15 minutes

Trace and cut out the locomotive and tender templates on page 94. Grease 2 cookie sheets. Roll out the cookie dough on a lightly floured surface. Lay the templates over the dough and, using a small, sharp knife or scalpel, cut around them. (Cut out one locomotive-shaped cookie for every three tender-shaped ones.) Place on the cookie sheets, spacing them slightly apart, and re-roll the trimmings to make extras. Bake in a preheated oven, 350°F, for 15 minutes or until pale golden. Using a spatula, transfer to a wire rack to cool.

Halve the butter frosting and stir a little food coloring into one half. Place the mixtures in 2 separate pastry bags fitted with star tips.

Use the uncolored frosting to pipe outlines around the cookies. Position large round candies for wheels and secure with frosting. Pipe more frosting over the curved tops of the tenders and scatter with small candies.

Use the colored frosting to pipe additional decorations onto the cookies. Pipe a dot of icing onto each wheel and secure a length of lace from one wheel center to the next. Arrange the cookies in lines across the party table so that each locomotive has three tenders arranged behind it.

cars

butter, for greasing

1 quantity Vanilla Cookie dough, chilled
  (see page 11)

flour, for dusting

4 oz white ready-to-use icing

confectioners' sugar, for dusting

1 tube yellow decorator frosting

double quantity Butter Frosting
  (see page 17)

a few drops of blue liquid or paste food
  coloring

large round candies for wheels

a selection of small candies

Makes 14–16

Preparation time: 1 hour, plus chilling

Cooking time: 15 minutes

The colors and shapes of these cookies are designed for younger children to make. Older children might prefer to design their own templates and styles of decoration.

Trace and cut out the car template on page 95. Grease 2 cookie sheets. Roll out the cookie dough on a lightly floured surface. Lay the template over the dough and, using a small, sharp knife or scalpel, cut around it. Place the shapes on the cookie sheets, spacing them slightly apart, and re-roll the trimmings to make extras. Bake in a preheated oven, 350°F, for 15 minutes or until pale golden. Using a spatula, transfer to a wire rack to cool.

Thinly roll out the white icing on a surface lightly dusted with confectioners' sugar and cut out small window shapes. Secure in place on the car shapes with a little decorator frosting from the tube. Use more decorator frosting to pipe outlines around the cookies.

Color the butter frosting with the food coloring and put it in a pastry bag fitted with a star tip. Use the frosting to pipe rounds for wheel tires and outlines around the windows.

Press the candies in place for wheels and finish decorating the cars with smaller candies. Pipe lines of yellow frosting over the wheel candies to represent spokes.

spots and stripes

butter, for greasing

1 quantity Spicy Gingerbread dough,
  chilled *(see page 10)*

flour, for dusting

3 oz milk chocolate, broken up

4 oz white ready-to-use icing

confectioners' sugar, for dusting

2 oz black ready-to-use icing

4 oz chocolate-flavored ready-to-use icing

5 oz yellow ready-to-use icing

2 oz light brown ready-to-use icing

Makes 24
Preparation time: 45 minutes, plus chilling
Cooking time: 15 minutes

These simple cookies are the easiest way to recreate the colors and patterns of kids' favorite safari animals, and are perfect for a theme party.

Grease 2 cookie sheets. Roll out the cookie dough on a lightly floured surface and, using a 3¼ inch round cookie cutter, cut out rounds. Place on the cookie sheets, spacing them slightly apart, and re-roll the trimmings to make extras. Bake in a preheated oven, 350°F, for 15 minutes or until the dough has risen slightly and is beginning to darken around the edges. Using a spatula, transfer to a wire rack to cool.

Melt the chocolate in a small bowl. Thinly roll out the white icing on a surface lightly dusted with confectioners' sugar. Roll very thin ropes of the black icing under the palms of your hands and lay them across the white at slightly irregular intervals. Use the rolling pin to gently roll the black icing into the white. Using a 2½ inch round cookie cutter, cut out 8 rounds. Spread one-third of the cookies with a little melted chocolate, then lay the rounds of icing over them.

Thinly roll out the chocolate-flavored icing. Use 2 oz of the yellow icing and the same technique as above to make 8 more stripy circles. Secure to 8 more cookies with melted chocolate.

Roll out the remaining yellow icing. Use the light brown icing to roll plenty of little balls in various sizes, then scatter them over the yellow icing. Gently roll with the rolling pin. Cut out 8 more rounds and secure to the remaining cookies with melted chocolate.

happy faces

butter, for greasing

1 quantity Vanilla Cookie dough, chilled
 (see page 11)

flour, for dusting

1 quantity Butter Frosting (see page 17)

4 tablespoons strawberry or raspberry jelly

Makes 16

Preparation time: 40 minutes, plus chilling

Cooking time: 15 minutes

Use a small cutter, about ½ inch in diameter, to cut out the eyes on these cookies. Alternatively, use the end of a large, plain piping tip.

Grease 2 cookie sheets. Roll out the cookie dough on a lightly floured surface and, using a 2½ inch round cookie cutter, cut out rounds. Place on the cookie sheets, spaced slightly apart, and re-roll the trimmings to make extras.

Cut out eyes (*see above*) in half the rounds, plus a large, smiling mouth, using a small, sharp knife or scalpel. Bake in a preheated oven, 350°F, for 15 minutes or until pale golden. Using a spatula, transfer to a wire rack to cool.

Spread the butter frosting over the plain cookies, then spread with the jelly. Gently press the face cookies on top.

decorated-hand cookies

butter, for greasing

1 quantity Vanilla Cookie dough, chilled
  (see page 11)

flour, for dusting

1 red food coloring pen

1 quantity Butter Frosting (see page 17)

a selection of small candies

edible silver or gold balls

Makes 10–15

Preparation time: 50 minutes, plus chilling

Cooking time: 15 minutes

Use a large hand-shaped cutter for these cookies, or, to make them really unique, get the children to make templates of their own hands. The amount of cookies made will depend on the size of the cutters or templates.

Grease 2 cookie sheets. Roll out the cookie dough on a lightly floured surface and use a cutter or template (*see above*) to cut out hand shapes. Place on the cookie sheets, spacing them slightly apart, and re-roll the trimmings to make extras. Bake in a preheated oven, 350°F, for 15 minutes or until pale golden. Using a spatula, transfer to a wire rack to cool.

Use the coloring pen to paint fingernails and any other decorations onto the cookies.

Put the butter frosting in a pastry bag fitted with a small star or writer tip. Use to secure the candies and silver or gold balls to the hands.

tropical fish

butter, for greasing

1 quantity Chocolate Cookie dough, chilled *(see page 11)*

flour, for dusting

a few drops of pink liquid or paste food coloring

1 quantity Butter Frosting *(see page 17)*

1 tablespoon bittersweet or milk chocolate chips

3 oz each of orange and yellow ready-to-use icing

confectioners' sugar, for dusting

Makes 16

Preparation time: 1 hour, plus chilling

Cooking time: 15 minutes

To make these cookies really effective, design your own fish-shaped templates in a couple of different shapes, or use a bought cookie cutter.

Grease 2 cookie sheets. Roll out the cookie dough on a lightly floured surface and, using a fish-shaped cutter or template, cut out fish shapes. Place on the cookie sheets, spacing them slightly apart, and re-roll the trimmings to make extras. Bake in a preheated oven, 350°F, for 15 minutes or until beginning to darken around the edges. Using a spatula, transfer to a wire rack to cool.

Beat the food coloring into the butter frosting and put it in a pastry bag fitted with a writer tip (or use a paper pastry bag and snip off the tip). Use the frosting to pipe tails, mouths, and eyes onto the fish shapes. Position a chocolate chip in the center of each eye.

Roll out the orange and yellow icings on a surface lightly dusted with confectioners' sugar. Cut out rounds and strips of icing, and secure to the fish with frosting. Finish with lines and dots of frosting.

lacy butterflies

butter, for greasing

1 quantity Vanilla Cookie dough, chilled
  (see page 11)

flour, for dusting

1 quantity Royal Icing *(see page 16)*

a few drops each of green and lilac liquid
  food coloring

2 tubes of pastel-colored glitter icing in
  contrasting shades

Makes 16

**Preparation time: 1¼ hours, plus chilling
  and setting**

Cooking time: 15 minutes

If you can't get hold of any glitter icing, pipe a thick, scalloped line of icing down the centers of the cookies and sprinkle with edible glitter.

Trace and cut out the butterfly template on page 95. Grease 2 cookie sheets. Roll out the cookie dough on a lightly floured surface. Lay the template over the dough and, using a small, sharp knife or scalpel, cut around it. Place on the cookie sheets, spacing them slightly apart, and re-roll the trimmings to make extras. Bake in a preheated oven, 350°F, for 15 minutes or until pale golden. Using a spatula, transfer to a wire rack to cool.

Put a little of the royal icing in a pastry bag fitted with a fine writer tip. Divide the remaining icing between 2 bowls. Add a few drops of green food coloring to one bowl and lilac to the other. Carefully stir a few drops of water into each one until the icing forms a flat surface when left to stand for 15 seconds.

Pipe a line of icing down the centers and around the edges of the cookies. Pipe circles of icing in the center of each wing and fill each circle with fine, wavy filigree lines. (These can be very irregular shapes as long as they match on the opposite wing.)

Using a small teaspoon, drizzle the green icing into the plain areas of half the cookies. Using a skewer, draw this to the edges at intervals (but don't fill in completely with icing). Repeat with the lilac icing on the remaining cookies. Leave in a cool place to set for about 1 hour or until the icing is just dry to the touch.

Pipe a thick band of glitter icing down the center of each butterfly.

bees and hives

butter, for greasing

1 quantity Chocolate Cookie dough, chilled
  (see page 11)

flour, for dusting

4 oz white chocolate, broken up

5 oz yellow ready-to-use icing

confectioners' sugar, for dusting

4 oz pale brown ready-to-use icing

1 oz white ready-to-use icing

bittersweet chocolate chips

2 sheets of rice paper

Makes 24

**Preparation time: 1 hour, plus chilling
  and setting**

Cooking time: 15 minutes

Even the simplest ideas can make really effective cookies. These colorful designs would be great for a kids' party in the garden.

Grease 2 cookie sheets. Roll out the cookie dough on a lightly floured surface. Cut out twelve 2½ inch rounds and place on the cookie sheets, spacing them slightly apart. Cut out 3 x 2 inch rectangles from the remaining dough, then round off one of the ends of each rectangle to make hive shapes. Re-roll the trimmings to make extras.

Bake in a preheated oven, 350°F, for 15 minutes or until just beginning to darken around the edges. Using a spatula, transfer to a wire rack to cool.

Melt the chocolate in a bowl and put it in a paper pastry bag. Snip off the tip.

Thinly roll out the yellow icing on a surface lightly dusted with confectioners' sugar. Cut out strips, about ½ inch wide, and lay them across the round cookies, securing with a little piped white chocolate. Trim off the excess icing around the edges of the cookies. Re-roll to make more strips.

Using a scribbling action, pipe more chocolate over the hive-shaped cookies. Thinly roll out the pale brown icing and cut into thin strips. Alternate strips of yellow and pale brown icing horizontally across the cookies. Trim off the excess icing, then cut out a small rectangle from the base of each one. Use the pale brown icing trimmings to shape and secure the bees' heads. Use the white icing and chocolate chips to make the eyes.

Cut each sheet of rice paper into 6 and fold the pieces in half lengthwise. Cut out a wing shape from each folded piece. Open out and secure to the bees by piping a line of chocolate down the back of each fold and gently pressing down onto each cookie. Leave in a cool place to set for about 1 hour.

puppies and kittens

butter, for greasing

1 quantity Chocolate Cookie dough, chilled
  (see page 11)

flour, for dusting

1 quantity Butter Frosting (see page 17)

6 oz pink ready-to-use icing

confectioners' sugar, for dusting

edible silver or gold balls

2 oz pale brown ready-to-use icing

6 oz blue ready-to-use icing

6 oz chocolate-flavored ready-to-use icing

1 tube black writer icing

Makes 20

Preparation time: 1 hour, plus chilling

Cooking time: 15 minutes

Grease a large cookie sheet. Roll out the cookie dough on a lightly floured surface and, using a 3¼ inch round cookie cutter, cut out rounds. Place on the cookie sheet, spacing them slightly apart, and re-roll the trimmings to make extras. Bake in a preheated oven, 350°F, for 15 minutes or until beginning to darken around the edges. Using a spatula, transfer to a wire rack to cool. Put the frosting in a pastry bag fitted with a writer tip.

For kittens, shape 10 triangular pieces of pink icing for noses. Secure to the centers of half the cookies with frosting. Press 1¼ inch strips of pink icing to the base of the cookies. Stud with silver or gold balls to make collars. Shape pointed ears in pale brown icing and secure with frosting. Pipe features onto the faces, then add round eyes and bow ties made of blue icing. With the writer icing, draw a black line down the center of the eyes.

For puppies, shape 10 triangles of pale brown icing for noses. Secure to the centers of the cookies with frosting. Make collars in blue icing. Pipe features, then add ears, pink tongues, and brown eyes.

little dinos

butter, for greasing

1 quantity Vanilla Cookie dough, chilled
 (see page 11)

flour, for dusting

10 oz green ready-to-use icing

confectioners' sugar, for dusting

4 oz yellow ready-to-use icing

1 quantity Butter Frosting (see page 17)

1 bag white chocolate rainbow buttons

1 oz brown ready-to-use icing

Makes 20

Preparation time: 1 hour, plus chilling

Cooking time: 15 minutes

Dinosaurs provide endless fascination for children of all ages. These spiky-backed creatures are cute enough even for toddlers.

Grease 2 cookie sheets. Roll out the cookie dough on a lightly floured surface and, using a 4 inch round cookie cutter, cut out rounds. Cut each round in half. Place on the cookie sheets, spacing them slightly apart, and re-roll the trimmings to make extras. Bake in a preheated oven, 350°F, for 15 minutes or until pale golden. Using a spatula, transfer to a wire rack to cool.

Lightly knead the green icing on a surface lightly dusted with confectioners' sugar. Tear the yellow icing into pieces and dot the pieces over the green icing. Roll the lump of icing under the palms of your hands into a thick sausage. Fold it in half and roll again. Repeat the rolling and folding until the icing colors have marbled together.

Put the butter frosting in a pastry bag fitted with a writer tip (or use a paper pastry bag and snip off the tip). Thinly roll out the marbled icing. Lay a cookie over the icing and, using a small, sharp knife or scalpel, cut around it, adding a curled extension of icing in one corner for the tail.

Pipe a little frosting over the cookie and lay the marbled icing on top. Repeat with the remainder. Re-roll the icing trimmings and cut out small heads, marking mouths with the tip of a knife. Secure to the bodies with frosting. Shape and secure ears and feet.

Cut the chocolate buttons into triangular shapes and, using frosting, secure along the top edge of the body of each cookie, making the triangles smaller as you reach the tail end. Pipe eyes and claws with butter frosting. Shape and secure small balls of brown icing for the centers of the eyes.

seasonal cookies

valentine hearts

butter, for greasing

1 quantity Vanilla Cookie dough, chilled
  (see page 11)

flour, for dusting

1 quantity Royal Icing (see page 16)

1 quantity raspberry or strawberry Fruit
  Glaze (see page 17)

Makes 14–16

**Preparation time: 50 minutes, plus chilling,
  cooling, and setting**

Cooking time: 15 minutes

To ensure that the "feathered" decoration on these cookies is smooth and delicate, complete each cookie one at a time so that the icing doesn't start to form a crust before you've piped the fruit glaze.

Grease 2 cookie sheets. Roll out the cookie dough on a lightly floured surface and, using 3¼ inch and 2½ inch heart-shaped cookie cutters, cut out heart shapes in the 2 sizes. Then, using a 1¾ inch heart-shaped cutter, cut out the centers of the large hearts. Place on the cookie sheets, spacing them slightly apart, and re-roll the trimmings to make extras. Bake in a preheated oven, 350°F, for 15 minutes or until pale golden. Using a spatula, transfer to a wire rack to cool.

Put about a quarter of the royal icing in a pastry bag fitted with a writer tip and use to pipe outlines around the edges of the heart shapes and a further line around the cut-out heart centers.

Put the fruit glaze in a pastry bag fitted with a writer tip (or use a paper pastry bag and snip off the tip).

Add a few drops of water to the remaining icing so that it forms a flat surface when left to stand for 15 seconds. Transfer the icing to a paper pastry bag. Snip off the tip and use the icing to "flood" the heart shapes, easing it to the edges with a toothpick. While the icing is still soft, pipe lines of fruit glaze over it, then draw a toothpick over the surface to "feather" the glaze into the icing. Leave in a cool place to set for at least 2 hours.

mothers' day flowers

butter, for greasing

1 quantity Vanilla Cookie dough, chilled
  (see page 11)

flour, for dusting

1 egg white, lightly beaten

10–12 wooden popsicle sticks

1 quantity Butter Frosting (see page 17)

a selection of fine and coarse pastel-
  colored sugar sprinkles

Makes 10–12

Preparation time: 1 hour, plus chilling

Cooking time: 15 minutes

Grease 2 cookie sheets. Thinly roll out the cookie dough on a lightly floured surface and, using a 2 inch rose petal cutter, cut out petals. Re-roll the trimmings to make extras.

Lightly brush the back of one petal with egg white and press it over a popsicle stick, set on a cookie sheet, with the point of the dough ½ inch from the end of the stick. Overlap 4 more petals to make a flower, brushing the overlapping areas with egg white to secure.

Bake in a preheated oven, 350°F, for 15 minutes or until pale golden. Leave on the cookie sheets to cool for 5 minutes, then, using a spatula, transfer to a wire rack.

Put the butter frosting in a pastry bag fitted with a small star tip and pipe a loop of icing onto each petal. Scatter with fine sugar sprinkles, tipping off the excess.

Pipe plenty of small stars into the center of the flowers and scatter with coarse sugar sprinkles. Tip off the excess.

easter nests

3 tablespoons unsalted butter, plus extra
  for greasing
1 quantity Chocolate Cookie dough, chilled
  (see page 11)
flour, for dusting
8 oz bittersweet chocolate, broken up
2 tablespoons corn syrup
2 cups shredded wheat breakfast cereal
plenty of candy-coated mini chocolate
  eggs

Makes about 20
**Preparation time: 40 minutes, plus chilling
  and setting**
Cooking time: 15 minutes

Grease 2 cookie sheets. Roll out the cookie dough on a lightly floured surface and, using a 2½ inch round cookie cutter, cut out rounds. Place on the cookie sheets, spacing them slightly apart, and bake in a preheated oven, 350°F, for about 15 minutes or until they are beginning to darken around the edges. Using a spatula, transfer to a wire rack to cool.

Put the chocolate in a small saucepan with the butter and corn syrup and heat very gently, stirring until the chocolate and butter have melted. Crumble the cereal into pieces, add it to the melted chocolate mixture and stir until completely coated.

Place spoonfuls of the mixture on the cookies, spreading it to the edges and making a dip in the centers to resemble nest shapes. Scatter 2 or 3 eggs into each nest and leave in a cool place to set for about 1 hour.

fall cookies

butter, for greasing

1 quantity Vanilla Cookie dough, chilled
  (see page 11)

flour, for dusting

double quantity Royal Icing *(see page 16)*

a few drops each of orange, yellow, and
  green liquid or paste food colorings

Makes 18–20

**Preparation time: 1¼ hours, plus chilling
  and setting**

Cooking time: 15 minutes

If you haven't any suitable cutters, trace shapes from pictures or real leaves and cut them out and use as templates. The pumpkin (including its stalk) and acorn should be 4 inches in height, and the leaf 5 inches.

Grease 2 cookie sheets. Roll out the cookie dough on a lightly floured surface and, using cutters or cutting around templates (*see above*), cut out pumpkin, acorn, and leaf shapes. Place on the cookie sheets, spacing them slightly apart, and re-roll the trimmings to make extras.

Bake in a preheated oven, 350°F, for 15 minutes or until pale golden. Using a spatula, transfer to a wire rack to cool.

Spoon a little royal icing into a pastry bag fitted with a writer tip. Divide the remaining icing between 3 bowls. Beat a food coloring into each bowl of icing, then add a few drops of water to each so that the icing forms a flat surface when left to stand for 15 seconds.

Brush the orange icing over the pumpkin shapes, leaving the stalks un-iced. Brush the leaves with the yellow icing, then brush yellow icing over the bases of the acorns. Brush the tops of the acorns with green icing. Pipe a thin line of icing from the writer tip around the cookies to finish and make decorative markings in the centers. Leave in a cool place to set for about 1 hour.

ghosties

butter, for greasing

1 quantity Vanilla Cookie dough, chilled
 (see page 11)

flour, for dusting

12 oz white ready-to-use icing

confectioners' sugar, for dusting

1 quantity Citrus Glaze *(see page 16)*

2 oz black ready-to-use icing

Makes 14–16

Preparation time: 50 minutes, plus chilling

Cooking time: 15 minutes

These Halloween spooks are effective, fun to make, and incredibly easy, as you can be fairly careless with the way you shape the ghostie outlines.

Trace and cut out 2 ghost templates on page 94, one template with eyes and mouth cut out and the other with just the ghost outline. Grease 2 cookie sheets. Roll out the cookie dough on a lightly floured surface. Lay the ghost outline template over the dough and, using a small, sharp knife or scalpel, cut around it. Place on the cookie sheets, spacing them slightly apart, and re-roll the trimmings to make extras. Bake in a preheated oven, 350°F, for 15 minutes or until pale golden. Using a spatula, transfer to a wire rack to cool.

Thinly roll out the white icing on a surface lightly dusted with confectioners' sugar. Lay the ghost template with features on the icing and, using a small, sharp knife or scalpel, cut around it. Then, using the knife or scalpel, cut out the eyes and mouth. Spread the cookies with a little citrus glaze and gently press the icing into position.

Roll the black icing into tiny pieces and press into the eye and mouth spaces.

shooting stars

butter, for greasing

1 quantity Spicy Gingerbread dough, chilled (see page 10)

flour, for dusting

1 quantity Royal Icing (see page 16)

a few drops each of orange and yellow liquid or paste food colorings

edible gold food coloring

Makes 24

Preparation time: 1 hour, plus chilling and setting

Cooking time: 15 minutes

Grease 2 cookie sheets. Roll out the dough on a lightly floured surface and, using a shooting star-shaped cookie cutter, cut out shapes. Place on the cookie sheets, spacing them slightly apart, and re-roll the trimmings to make extras. Bake in a preheated oven, 350°F, for 15 minutes or until the dough has risen slightly and is beginning to darken around the edges. Using a spatula, transfer to a wire rack to cool.

Divide the icing between 2 bowls and add the orange food coloring to one and yellow to the other. Place in 2 separate pastry bags fitted with writer tips (or use paper pastry bags and snip off the tips).

Use the icing to pipe star-shaped outlines and broken lines of piping on the tails of the stars. Leave in a cool place to set for about 30 minutes. Use the gold food coloring to paint highlights over the cookies.

candy canes

butter, for greasing

1 quantity Vanilla Cookie dough, chilled
  (see page 11)

flour, for dusting

sugar sprinkles in red and green

1 quantity apricot Fruit Glaze (see page 17)

1 quantity Royal Icing (see page 16)

Makes 28–30

**Preparation time: 50 minutes, plus chilling
  and setting**

Cooking time: 15 minutes

Hang these on the Christmas tree. To make the template, draw a walking stick, ½ inch wide and 4 inches long, with a curved end.

Grease 2 cookie sheets. Roll out the cookie dough on a lightly floured surface. Lay the template over the dough and, using a small, sharp knife or scalpel, cut around it.

Place the shapes on the cookie sheets, spacing them slightly apart, and re-roll the trimmings to make extras. Bake in a preheated oven, 350°F, for 15 minutes or until pale golden. Transfer to a wire rack to cool.

Brush the cookies with the fruit glaze. Scatter thin bands of red and green sugar sprinkles over the cookies, leaving small gaps between the colors.

Put the icing in a pastry bag fitted with a writer tip and pipe a line of icing between the sugars and round the edge to finish. Leave the cookies in a cool place to set for at least 1 hour before hanging them on the tree.

snowflakes

butter, for greasing

1 quantity Vanilla Cookie dough, chilled
  (see page 11)

flour, for dusting

double quantity Citrus Glaze (see page 16)

1 quantity Royal Icing (see page 16)

fine ribbon, for threading

Makes 14

**Preparation time: 50 minutes, plus chilling
  and setting**

Cooking time: 15 minutes

These make stunning Christmas tree cookies, especially if you make plenty of them. Don't forget to re-shape the holes for threading the ribbon as soon as they come out of the oven.

***

Grease 2 cookie sheets. Roll out the cookie dough on a lightly floured surface and, using a 4 inch star cookie cutter (measured from point to point), cut out star shapes. Put on the cookie sheets, spacing them slightly apart, and re-roll the trimmings to make extras. Using a skewer, make a small hole near the tip of one point of each star for threading the ribbon. Bake in a preheated oven, 350°F, for 15 minutes or until pale golden. Remove from the oven and immediately re-mark the holes, as the dough will have risen slightly during baking. Using a spatula, transfer to a wire rack to cool.

Using a teaspoon, spread the citrus glaze over the cookies, spreading it almost to the edges.

Put the royal icing in a pastry bag fitted with a writer tip. Pipe 3 lines across each cookie—start from opposite points so that they cross in the center. Pipe a row of tiny chevrons over each line to resemble snowflakes. Leave in a cool place to set for at least 1 hour before threading with ribbon.

3D winter wonderland

butter, for greasing

double quantity Spicy Gingerbread dough,
  chilled *(see page 10)*

flour, for dusting

1 quantity Royal Icing *(see page 16)*

4 oz red ready-to-use icing

confectioners' sugar, for dusting

1 oz black ready-to-use icing

colorful wrapped candies to fill sleigh
  (optional)

Makes 1 winter scene

Preparation time: about 1½ hours,
  plus chilling and setting

Cooking time: 15 minutes

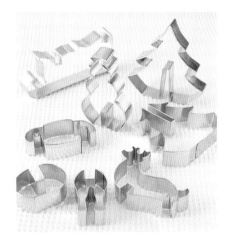

For this 3D winter wonderland you'll need to make your own templates of deer, a sleigh, tree, and snowman or buy a set of cutters like the one used here.

Grease 3 large cookie sheets. Roll out the cookie dough on a lightly floured surface and cut out shapes using templates or cookie cutters. You will need 2 sleigh sides, 2 sleigh ends, 2 reindeer bodies and 4 pairs of legs, 1 snowman with base, and 1 tree with base. Place on the cookie sheets, spacing them slightly apart, and re-roll the trimmings to make extra trees for a wonderland "forest" and a few spares in case of breakage.

Bake in a preheated oven, 350°F for 15 minutes or until the dough has risen slightly and is beginning to darken around the edges. Leave on the cookie sheets for 5 minutes, then transfer to wire racks to cool.

Put the royal icing in a pastry bag fitted with a writer tip. Thinly roll out the red icing on a surface dusted with confectioners' sugar and cut out 4 top sections for the sleigh sides using a template or cutter. Secure in place using a little icing from the bag. Roll out the black icing and cut out small squares for the reindeers' hooves. Shape and secure small red noses. Shape and secure a red scarf and black hat for the snowman.

Use the icing in the bag to pipe decorations on the sleigh, reindeer, snowman, and tree. Leave to set for at least 1 hour.

Assemble the scene by slotting the pieces together. Dust lightly with confectioners' sugar, if desired, and fill the sleigh with candies, if using.

christmas baubles

butter, for greasing

1 quantity Vanilla Cookie dough, chilled
  (see page 11)

flour, for dusting

2 tablespoons egg white

a few drops each of orange and green
  liquid food colorings (or colors of your
  choice)

white sugar sprinkles

1 quantity Royal Icing *(see page 16)*

fine ribbon, for threading

Makes 20

**Preparation time: 1 hour, plus chilling
  and setting**

Cooking time: 15 minutes

**These cookies make a fabulous alternative to conventional bauble
decorations for hanging on the Christmas tree, and give you the flexibility
of choosing your own color scheme.**

Grease 2 cookie sheets. Roll out the cookie dough on a lightly floured
surface and, using a 3¼ inch round cookie cutter, cut out rounds. Place on
the cookie sheets, spacing them slightly apart, and re-roll the trimmings to
make extras.

Using a skewer, make a small hole about ½ inch from the edge of each
circle for threading the ribbon. Bake in a preheated oven, 350°F, for
15 minutes or until pale golden. Remove from the oven and immediately
re-mark the holes, as the dough will have risen slightly during baking.
Using a spatula, transfer to a wire rack to cool.

Beat the egg white to break it up and divide between 2 small dishes. Add
the orange coloring to one and the green to the other. Use a fine paintbrush
to paint designs over each cookie, then scatter with sugar sprinkles.

Put the royal icing in a pastry bag fitted with a small star tip. Pipe a line
of icing between the sugars and round the edges of the cookies to finish.
Leave in a cool place to set for at least 1 hour before threading with ribbon
for hanging.

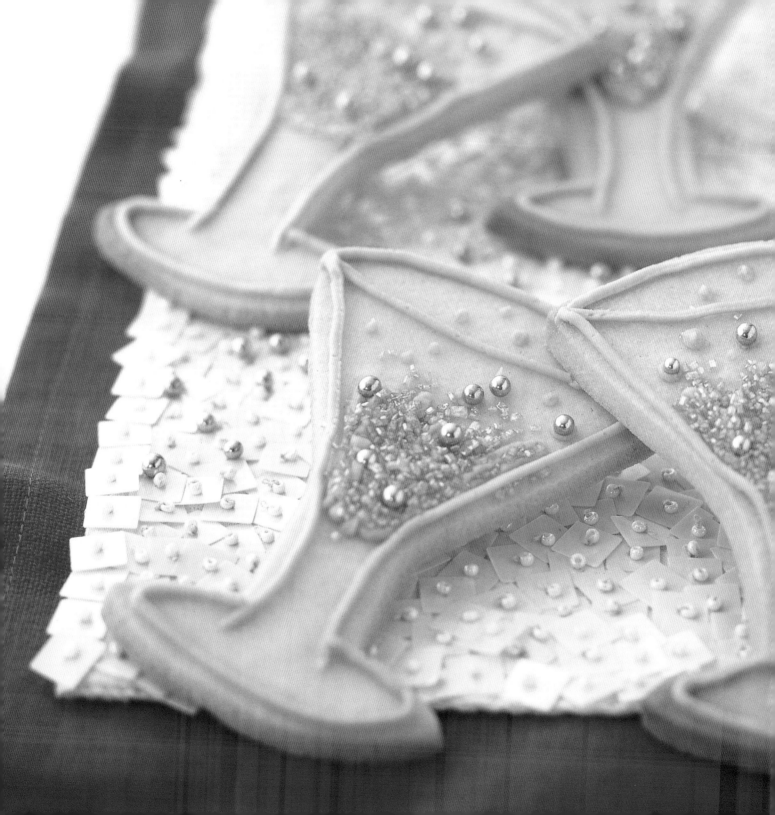

special occasion
cookies

gingerbread nightlights

1 quantity Spicy Gingerbread dough, chilled *(see page 10)*

flour, for dusting

6 oz colored boiled candies

1 quantity Royal Icing *(see page 16)*

4 nightlights

Makes 4

Preparation time: 50 minutes, plus chilling and setting

Cooking time: 15 minutes

Dim the lights and bring an atmospheric glow to a special-occasion table with these stunning centerpieces. They're best made just a day in advance, as the candies will gradually soften when exposed to the air.

Line 2 cookie sheets with parchment paper. On a lightly floured surface, thinly roll out half the cookie dough large enough from which to cut out a neat 14 x 7 inch rectangle. Carefully lift onto one cookie sheet and trim the edges to make the rectangle. Using a ruler, cut the dough into 8 exact 3½ inch squares.

Using a 3¼ inch star cutter (measured from point to point), cut out a star shape from each square. The star shapes that you've cut out from the centers can be cooked and decorated separately if desired. Repeat with the second batch of dough on the second cookie sheet.

Bake the squares in a preheated oven, 350°F, for 5 minutes. While they are baking, use a rolling pin or small hammer to lightly crush the candies in their wrappers. Remove the cookie sheets from the oven and scatter the crushed candies into the cut-out star areas. Return to the oven for an additional 8–10 minutes until the gingerbread is lightly colored and the candies have melted to fill the stars. (If they haven't completely spread into the corners, use a wooden skewer to spread the syrup while it is still soft.) Re-cut the edges of the cookie squares, as they will have merged together a little during baking, then leave on the cookie sheets to cool.

Put the icing in a pastry bag fitted with a writer tip. Pipe a line of icing down one inside edge of 4 cookies and secure together to make 4 sides of a box shape. Make 3 more box shapes. Use the remaining icing in the bag to pipe decorative lines around the edges of the boxes. Leave in a cool place to set for at least 2 hours.

When ready to use, light a nightlight and lower a gingerbread box over it. (If the nightlight is going to be lit for some while, protect the table with a little mat or coaster underneath the nightlight.)

birthday bundles

butter, for greasing

1 quantity Spicy Gingerbread dough, chilled *(see page 10)*

flour, for dusting

1 quantity Citrus Glaze *(see page 16)*

different-colored sugar sprinkles

fine ribbon, in 2 colors, for wrapping bundles

Makes 12 cookies (4 bundles)

Preparation time: 50 minutes, plus chilling and setting

Cooking time: 18 minutes

Grease a large cookie sheet. Roll out the cookie dough on a lightly floured surface and transfer the dough to the cookie sheet. Cut off the rough edges, but leave them in position to keep the dough in place. Cut out an equal amount of squares and rectangles from the dough, making the rectangles about 3¼ x 1¾ inches and the squares 2 inches.

Bake the shapes in a preheated oven, 350°F, for 16–18 minutes or until the dough has risen slightly and is beginning to darken around the edges. Re-cut the marked lines and transfer the cookies to a wire rack to cool.

Line a tray or cleaned cookie sheet with parchment paper. Using a teaspoon, drizzle wavy lines of citrus glaze over the top of a cookie, then brush more around the sides. Scatter with sugar sprinkles, tipping off the excess, then dip the sides in sugar sprinkles. Transfer the cookie to the parchment paper. Repeat with the remaining cookies then leave them in a cool place to set for 2 hours.

Stack the cookies in little bundles and tie with ribbon.

pink champagne cocktails

butter, for greasing

1 quantity Vanilla Cookie dough, chilled
  (see page 11)

flour, for dusting

a few drops of pink liquid or paste food
  coloring

1 quantity Butter Frosting *(see page 17)*

sugar sprinkles

pink-tinted silver balls

Makes 16

Preparation time: 45 minutes, plus chilling

Cooking time: 15 minutes

These celebratory cookies will add a stylish touch to a variety of special occasions, from a 21st birthday to an engagement party. Trace and cut out a cocktail glass shape from a picture, about 4 x 3¼ inches, and use as a template.

Grease 2 cookie sheets. Roll out the cookie dough on a lightly floured surface. Lay the template over the dough and, using a small, sharp knife or scalpel, cut around it. Place on the cookie sheets, spacing them slightly apart, and re-roll the trimmings to make extras. Bake in a preheated oven, 350°F, for 15 minutes or until pale golden. Using a spatula, transfer to a wire rack to cool.

Beat the food coloring into the butter frosting and put half in a pastry bag fitted with a writer tip (or use a paper pastry bag and snip off the tip). Using a spatula, spread a little frosting across the center of the cookies so that they look like half-filled glasses. Pipe an outline of frosting around the edges of the cookies. Scatter the glass cavity area with sugar sprinkles. Pipe dots of frosting to resemble bubbles and sprinkle with pink-tinted silver balls.

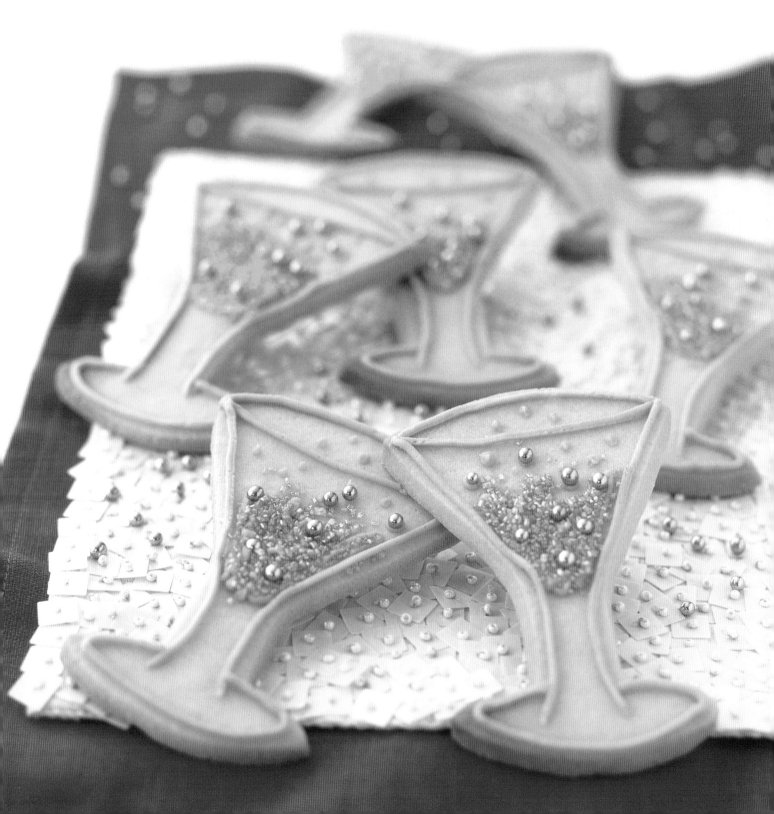

wise old owls

butter, for greasing

1 quantity Vanilla Cookie dough, chilled
  (see page 11)

flour, for dusting

1 tablespoon egg white, lightly beaten

2 teaspoons cocoa powder

1 teaspoon water

1 quantity Royal Icing *(see page 16)*

2 oz each of white, blue, and yellow
  ready-to-use icing

Makes 18

**Preparation time: 1¼ hours, plus chilling
  and setting**

Cooking time: 15 minutes

These fun cookies are perfect for graduation day celebrations. Don't forget to paint the biscuits with cocoa paste before baking them.

Trace and cut out the owl template on page 95. Grease 2 cookie sheets. Roll out the cookie dough on a lightly floured surface. Lay the template over the dough and, using a small, sharp knife or scalpel, cut around it. Place on the cookie sheets, spacing them slightly apart, and re-roll the trimmings to make extras.

Beat together the egg white, cocoa powder, and water to make a smooth, thin paste. Using a fine paintbrush, paint the wing, head, and beak areas on the owls. Bake in a preheated oven, 350°F, for 15 minutes or until pale golden. Using a spatula, transfer to a wire rack to cool.

Put the royal icing in a pastry bag fitted with a writer tip. Use the white ready-to-use icing to shape round eyes, then secure them in place with a little royal icing from the bag. Use the blue icing to shape centers for the eyes, then secure with royal icing. Cut out feet shapes in yellow icing and secure in place. Use the icing left in the bag to paint the wing and breast feathers. Leave in a cool place to set for about 1 hour.

place names

butter, for greasing

1 quantity Vanilla Cookie dough, chilled
  (see page 11)

flour, for dusting

plenty of fine, colored ribbon, for threading

1 quantity Royal Icing *(see page 16)*

Makes 10

**Preparation time: 50 minutes, plus chilling
  and setting**

Cooking time: 15 minutes

Grease 2 cookie sheets. Roll out the cookie dough on a lightly floured surface and cut out ten 3¾ x 3 inch rectangles. Place on the cookie sheets, spacing them slightly apart. Using the end of a teaspoon, make 12 wide cuts in an oval shape around the middle of each cookie so that the ribbon can be threaded through after baking.

Bake in a preheated oven, 350°F, for 15 minutes or until pale golden. Remove from the oven and re-mark the cuts. Using a spatula, transfer to a wire rack to cool.

Thread the cookies with ribbon, leaving the ends untied.

Put the icing in a pastry bag fitted with a writer tip. With the untied ends of ribbon farthest from you, pipe names across the cookies.

Use the remaining icing to pipe decorative borders around the edges of the cookies. Leave to set for 1–2 hours. Tie the ribbon ends in bows and cut off any excess.

baby shower cookies

butter, for greasing

1 quantity Vanilla Cookie dough, chilled
(see page 11)

flour, for dusting

1 quantity Royal Icing (see page 16)

5 pink jelly beans, halved lengthwise

3 oz pale blue, pink, or yellow ready-to-use
icing

10 small blue, pink, or yellow bows

Makes 20

**Preparation time: 1 hour, plus chilling
and setting**

Cooking time: 15 minutes

Feeding bottles and baby booties are just two appropriate designs for a baby shower party. Other ideas on the same theme might include diapers, rattles, or building blocks.

Trace and cut out the bootie and bottle templates on pages 94 and 95. Grease 2 cookie sheets. Roll out the cookie dough on a lightly floured surface. Lay the templates over the dough and, using a small, sharp knife or scalpel, cut around them. Place on the cookie sheets, spacing them slightly apart, and re-roll the trimmings to make extras. Bake in a preheated oven, 350°F, for 15 minutes or until pale golden. Using a spatula, transfer to a wire rack to cool.

Put a little of the royal icing in a pastry bag fitted with a fine writer tip. Carefully add a few drops of water to the remaining icing until the icing forms a flat surface when left to stand for 15 seconds.

Pipe a line of icing around the edges of the cookies. Pipe a line of circles across the ankles of the booties and a diagonal line of piping across the center of the bottles. Using a small teaspoon, drizzle a little of the thinned icing onto the lower part of the bottles, spreading it to the edges with the back of a teaspoon and easing it into the corners with a toothpick. Spread the icing onto the bootie-shaped cookies in the same way, easing it around the piping across the ankles.

Secure a jelly bean half, cut side down, to the top of each bottle with a little icing. Shape a little band of ready-to-use icing and secure around the neck of the bottles.

Leave the cookies in a cool place to set for about 30 minutes or until the royal icing is dry to the touch, then pipe wavy lines onto the booties and over the ready-to-use icing on the bottles. Secure the bows to the booties with a dot of royal icing. Leave to set again for 30 minutes.

templates

All templates should be enlarged
by 125 percent.

ghosties
pages 70–71

baby shower cookies
pages 92–93

steam trains
pages 44–45

steam trains
pages 44–45

shoes and purses
pages 34–35

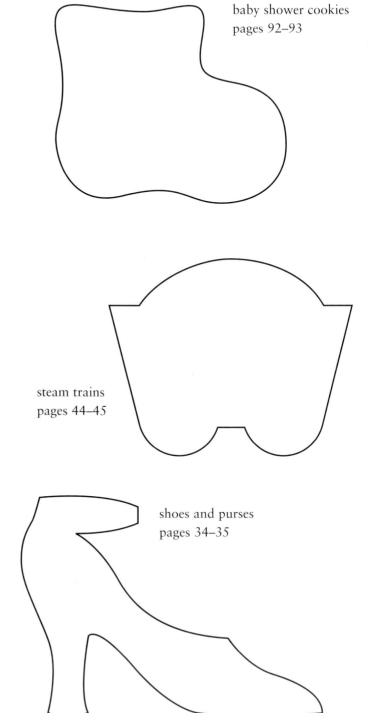

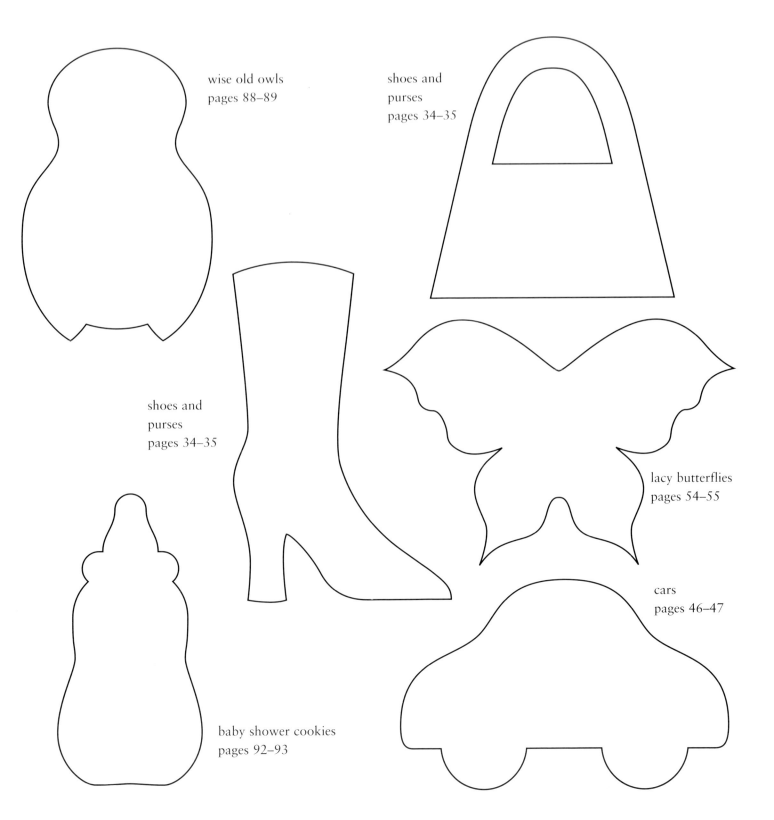

wise old owls
pages 88–89

shoes and
purses
pages 34–35

shoes and
purses
pages 34–35

lacy butterflies
pages 54–55

cars
pages 46–47

baby shower cookies
pages 92–93

index

acknowledgments

Photographer Lis Parsons
Home economist Joanna Farrow